Someday It'll All Be... Who's?

Léon Danco
Donald J. Jonovic

The Center for Family Business
Family Business Management Services
Cleveland

This book is a joint publication of The University Press, Post Office Box 24268, Cleveland, Ohio 44124 and Jamieson Press, Post Office Box 909, Cleveland, Ohio 44120.

Library of Congress Cataloging-in-Publication Data

Danco, Léon A., 1923-
Someday, It'll All Be...Who's? / Léon A. Danco, Donald J. Jonovic.
p.   cm.
ISBN 0-9603614-5-6 (University): $24.95
ISBN 0-915607-09-3 (Jamieson): $24.95
1. Family-owned business enterprises—Caricatures and cartoons.
2. American wit and humor, Pictorial.
I. Jonovic, Donald J., 1943-.
II. Title
NC 1429.D2344A4 1990
741.5'973—dc20
90-49915
CIP

First printing: November 1990
Printed in the U.S.A.

ACKNOWLEDGEMENT

The existence of this book, to a great extent, is due to the cooperation of King Features Syndicate, Inc., original distributor of the majority of the cartoons on these pages. We particularly wish to thank Ita Golzman, Director of Domestic Licensing at King, for her cooperation and support. Her open mind and foresight early in the process allowed the project to begin, and she made the development process efficient and enjoyable.

PREFACE

It only hurts when we don't laugh.

This simple truth is one of the major lessons we've learned in our combined experience of almost 50 years working with families in business.

Fact is, surviving success in one's own businesss is *serious* business. The challenges that come with growth, management transition, and expanding ownership of family companies can be daunting. Even when the whole process goes as it should, the day-to-day effort of working through the important issues can be stress-filled and exhausting.

There is good reason to stick with it, however. As we've said many times, ownership of a happy , successful family business can be the best economic way of life Western man has produced. Smooth growth and generational transition with minimum tension may be tough to achieve, but the end result is well worth the sweat and pain.

This book is the outgrowth of an abiding interest each of us has in the power of humor as a lubricant in the process of understanding family businesses and the people in them. It's almost impossible to be involved in the serious and stressful issues of survival and succession without the relief of humor. Laughter is a great lever for increasing mutual understanding and raising sensitivity.

Proof, for us, of humor's importance in the survival and growth of family companies has been the ongoing exchange of cartoons between us and our clients over the years. It seems that once exposed to a good gag, business owners (and family business advisors, for that matter) find it impossible not to make copies for friends and colleagues around the country. In fact, this natural "cartoon exchange" became so great that we soon began to fill file folders to overflowing.

Through it all, an idea formed in the back of our minds. The concept of this book came up between us every few years, but never really got off the ground. The logistics of copyright were immense and daunting, and there were so many other projects to absorb our time and attention.

It wasn't until we were fortunate enough to find a cartoon syndicate with enough foresight and understanding to give us access to their archives -- and permission to reprint their cartoons with a minimum of red tape -- that we were able to make this project a reality. Credit for the publication of this collection must go as much to King Features as to us.

We urge you to use this book as it was meant to be used. Dip in and out. Open it when you feel the need for a healthy chuckle. Share it with others who will understand. Maybe even use it as a gentle prod to begin taking some necessary steps. We've tried not to spare anyone from the "invigorating" barb of humor, and we've not pulled too many punches (although the gloves, you'll find, are heavily padded).

These "insider" jokes contain as much truth and understanding as the most "definitive" conventional book about family business. That's why collecting and editing these cartoons has been such a fascinating and enjoyable process for us. We hope that reading and sharing them with us will be just as therapeutic for you.

Welcome to the lighter side of the *real* world of family business.

LAD
DJJ

Someday, Son, this will all be yours — assuming I can get my father to give it to me.

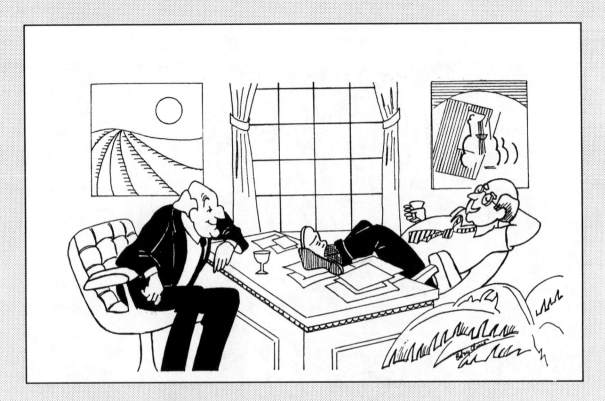

Of course I'm enjoying myself. Where else in the world could I be both irresistible force *and* immovable object?

Somehow, the whole idea of starting a business dynasty is losing a lot of its luster.

...And after Mildred proposed that the average of the three valuations be submitted to the original valuation firm's astrologist for comparison against the departing shareholder's third notarized offer, how did each of you feel about signing the buy/sell agreement?

It's okay. Nobody showed up.

But I'd always kind of assumed that the one
inevitability cancelled out the other.

Sure beats Junior League, doesn't it?

Oh, you hear a lot about the wonders of inheriting a family business, but nobody ever talks about how *long* it takes.

I'm so pleased to see that all of you decided to bring your own attorneys.

I take it, then, that opinion is divided along family lines?

Your brother's wife came by today in their new company Mercedes.

Danco / Jonovic — Someday It'll All Be...Who's?

I was thinking today, Charles, that vast sums of inherited money have been very good to us.

Maybe Dad DID know something we didn't...

Danco / Jonovic — Someday It'll All Be...Who's?

That happens to Dad's portrait every time the
monthly financials cross my desk.

Someday, Son, this will all be yours — any resulting
child abuse charges be damned.

Dream all the impossible dreams you want, but remember who's the unbeatable foe around here.

We took the afternoon off from the office to come
cheer you up, Dad.

Oh, for heaven's sake, George, if you can't relax, go ahead and have them send you the financial statements every month!

Well, maybe you *should* have held onto the stock, but staring north for hours isn't going to bring it back.

I know it's Dad's business, and the buck doesn't stop here, but I wish it would pass through this neighborhood once in a while.

It's from The Boss. His son will be working in the plant this summer, and he wants us all to remember that the kid was raised by his mother.

Mr. Evans, meet Harry Thomas. He has
inactive family shareholders, too.

Well, by darn, you're right. Why worry about a career when you can work for your dad?

...Then one day I figured I'd had enough. I go into my Dad's office and I say: "Look, Dad, this business ain't big enough for both of us. One of us has gotta go..."

What a fool I was. I thought money could make one happy. I didn't even *begin* to realize how happy...

If you can't find him, at least help me find his
buy/sell agreement!

Danco / Jonovic — Someday It'll All Be...Who's?

Who says your brother's the most logical choice as
the next president?

Why simplify the tax code? If we just eliminate the
deductibility of professional fees, the deficit will
disappear in six months.

It's my ex-wife's annual comment on the year-end dividends.

Dad had a kind of blunt management style, but it worked.

I'm sorry, Mr. Kingsley, but it seems your heirs read your will and cancelled your reservation.

Someday, Son, this will all be yours — except for
Ms. Flamebody. She stays with me.

Fellow senators! I propose we simply nationalize
American business and get it over with.

Your raise was based solely on continued performance, Smedly, specifically the birth of my only daughter's second son.

Hey, don't worry about an employment contract,
Baxter. Just do everything my way, and I'll take
care of you like I would my son.

Business owners aren't supposed to get ulcers, Mr. Findley. They're supposed to *give* them.

It's hard to manage a kid young enough to be your son, and rich enough not to have to listen.

My son's joining the company. Design a job that sounds important, with no duties that could interfere with operations.

This job's too dirty for any real employee, Son, so we're giving it to you for the summer.

Keep making mistakes like this, Son, and I'll
have to fire someone.

Someday, Honey, this will all be your brother's.

I think I need an editor from <u>Inc.</u> Magazine to
airbrush my entrepreneurial image.

Well, at the moment, I feel like a minority
shareholder with a tax problem in the
middle of a divorce.

Someday, Son, this will all be yours – and, of course, your mother's, your sisters', your cousin Jimmie Joe's, the Heart Society...

Well, look at it this way, Mr. Miller. Your sisters finally agreed on something — even if it was only the same lawyer.

They're playing "Shareholders"!

In response to your business advice, my Dear, I'd remind you that what exists between you and my son is a marriage — not a merger.

She mated the head judge's rottweiler.

It's about time we took over
our independent distributors
— assuming they're willing
to take their old jobs back.

We should encourage the
survival of family
businesses — bigger
suppliers wouldn't put up
with 120-day payment.

I don't know why your children are upset, Alan.
Lots of business owners marry their secretaries.

Your success will be due to years of
struggle, terrifying risk, and massive
sacrifices — mine.

Now, don't be evolving into anything while we're
in Florida.

As a matter of fact, my father *does* own a
business. Why do you ask?

So, how was the tax seminar?

Every time he gets cranky and irritable, just take two of these and remind him you never wanted him to retire in the first place.

You knew him as vigorous, sculptured, and
enduringly impeccable. Since he sold the business,
I know him as a shapeless blob.

The good news is your buy/sell agreement is already funded with life insurance.

Actually, he doesn't have a job. He works for my father.

You've been like a father to me, Mr. Fletchley —
distant, demanding, and unresponsive.

Gentlemen, I would prefer that you stop referring to my inheriting the company as "J.B.'s little joke on the family."

Looks like the boss can't find a buyer. He's talking about forming an ESOP.

Someday, Son, this will all be yours – unless I
can come up with a better solution.

Your father says that's the way it *is*. You *are* all desk and no authority.

As a final, desperate strategy, I've decided to put all directors on straight commission.

We're *not* trying to manage your life, Son, but when you grow up, we do sort of expect you to be a penguin.

Danco / Jonovic — Someday It'll All Be...Who's?

"...and since my family always thought I had money to burn, I had it cremated with me."

Before you say anything, Son, I had good reason to veto your reorganization plan. Also, in the future, you can skip the dramatizations...

Well, my boy, you can tell me. How much did business fall off during my four months in Ft. Myers?

Waddya mean, you want it *now*?

Onto *that* my failing hands are supposed to pass the torch...

You tell my son he can't put me on the list of people he refuses to see — I'm his boss.

Danco / Jonovic — Someday It'll All Be...Who's?

Your future, my Son, lies where your father owns a majority of the shares.

Your Dad wants to discuss that company
Ferrari you bought while he was gone.

Well, it's official, gentlemen. We now have 1.3 family business consultants for every man, woman, and child in the United States.

Shock? Waddya mean, "shock"? All I said was that he handled
the Pendergast problem much better than I could have.

Your Father's expecting you.

Well, my son finally contributed something to a board meeting. Yesterday he "waived the movement of the last minute's readings."

I take it asking for my daughter's hand in "merger" was a Freudian slip...

Someday, Son, this will all be yours — so don't marry an environmentalist.

Are the tax
inspectors
supposed to
see this other
set of books?

I'm telling them
no bonuses this
year, and you have
to walk in with
that coat!

I couldn't strike terror into anyone's heart out there...What's going on around here?

We've got a problem. My grandchildren won't go along with the recapitalization.

Inheriting the business from you makes me a
born businessman, right, Dad?

It's something I find very soothing — my son's
prenuptial agreement.

We made it shirtsleeves to shirtsleeves in *one* generation.

Dad, I think I deserve a bigger salary —
and, incidently, so does your wife.

Danco / Jonovic — Someday It'll All Be...Who's?

We've got our payables up to 120 days.
Father would've been so proud of me.

So, this is the old workshop, eh, Don?

Stop complaining. At least you get *paid* to put up with him.

Burned out, Son? How could that be?
I wasn't aware you'd ever ignited.

If I have to inherit the business someday, I'm not so sure I *want* to grow up.

No. I don't think there's been a mistake.
You *are* a lawyer, aren't you?

There, there, now — I'm sure your father will
let you retire someday.

Well...you tell me. Would *you* lend money to
anyone who needs it as badly as you do?

Someday, Son, you will try to rip all this
out of my grasp.

Look, Mabel! Buried treasure!

I hate to tell you this, Billy, but there won't be
any dividend this summer. We have to invest
in a new lemon.

That's the senior litigator at Ketchum, Grabbit and
Runnion who married Mabel's 20%. I think he's
sending a signal to the rest of us.

In *my* company, it's the first mate who goes down with the ship, *not* the captain!

For years I've looked forward to retirement,
but not in this body.

Once again, the genius and wisdom of majority rule is demonstrated.

Danco / Jonovic — Someday It'll All Be...Who's?

Post this immediately: "My statement in the company newsletter that we considered all our employees to be part of the family *was only a figure of speech!*"

As near as we can tell, the only thing keeping you alive is the realization that your son would inherit the business.

The Boss made the mistake of asking his wife to help out for a
few days while we were short-handed. That was 10 years ago.

I think old man McGuffy went a little too far trying to be fair to his boys.

Where were you when the really *big* fortunes
were being made, Daddy?

Tell your husband to relax. The child's obsession with Machiavelli, Macbeth, and Lucretia Borgia is just a phase.

I realize you left the business early so we could have this quality time together, but have we been introduced?

I just realized there's nothing more oppressive
than having a great future.

I just had a horrible thought. What if they all actually *came* to the shareholder meeting?

No, Bill, this is *not* a good time to discuss firing my brother.

That's right — a druggist with a corporate airplane. Boys, it doesn't get much better than this!

Someday, Son, this will all be yours — assuming your attorney is smarter than mine.

Nobody will ever understand what sacrifices I've had to make trying to build this business single-handedly.

You think he's upset about that cigarette butt on the plant floor? Wait'll he notices there's no toilet paper in the men's room.

My ex-wife lives there with my first business.

You just had to keep begging me to give you
that "one big chance," didn't you, Son?

It's your father at the office, mumbling something about
how *he* always *worked* Saturday nights.

Just out of curiosity, what's the
secret behind your drive?

Which one am I gonna
have to fight for control of
the business, Daddy?

He just creates the stuff.
It's up to me to sell it.

All I can do is repeat
what Mr. Wilson said.
Do you want him to run
the business or spend all
his time dealing with
disgruntled
shareholders?

Well, I know I was only supposed to hire an ordertaker, Dad, but after I hired Mary Jo, I discovered she couldn't type. So I hired Sue. But neither of them understands electronics, so I had to hire Stan to keep the product line straight. Now, it turns out all three of them are so disorganized we're losing orders. That's why we need a general manager.

Well, I think it was very sweet of Daddy
to name you Vice President of Parking.

Danco / Jonovic — Someday It'll All Be...Who's?

Okay, just for argument's sake, let's say I go for this...

Let's see, that's nine "ayes," one "what are we voting on?",
six "abstains," and one "go to hell."

My son's decided to join the company. See if you can keep him out of sight.

Quite frankly, Mr. Billingsly, nobody's ever listed "Dad's vague, evasive, unfulfilled promises" as a personal asset before.

You really impressed Dad at the office today.
I overheard him saying he never knew his
daughter-in-law had such a powerful right hook.

Okay. Good point...Junior can have his raise.

These, Son, are the shoes I'm hiring you to fill.

Just stop thinking of it as your money, and this'll go a lot easier for both of us.

Gotcha!

Like the swallows to Capistrano and the
buzzards to Hinckley...Dad's annual return
from Scottsdale.

Wearing the coat to the company Christmas party doesn't make it deductible, but I like your thinking, Dear.

I'm not *giving* this bride away, Reverend. It's
costing me $10,000, plus 10% of my stock.

Uh...I've been wondering, Dad. Just *when* is this "someday" you've been referring to?

Don't worry about me. If I don't make it out there,
there's always nepotism to fall back on.

Congratulations on your engagement to my
daughter, Bulgley. I presume, now, you'd like
to apply these impressive skills to my company.

Some women just never let go.

Someday, Son, you'll wish all this *wasn't* yours.

Denkins, if you want to get ahead in my company, you
have to *marry* my daughter, not just live with her.

Of course, tomorrow's papers will say you're "eagerly looking forward to retirement" and you turned the reins over to your son with "pride and confidence."

I thought you'd want to know — your father's out
raising hell in the plant again.

As you grow with our law firm, Wiggins,
I think you'll find that exhorbitant fees
will work for you.

Whatever he lacks in talent and drive, he more than makes up for by being The Boss's son.

Get my kids in here. I feel like rearing my ugly head.

But on the other hand, it can't buy
unhappiness either.

My accountant just phoned to tell
me I'm fully depreciated.

Someday, Son, this will all be yours — unless I can persuade Ms. Buxum to run away with me.

Jenkins, my son, here, is joining the company. See that what he learned in business school doesn't hurt us.

It has to qualify as the bloodiest management transition I ever witnessed.

He's worked for his father for 34 years.
What do you *think* is wrong with him?

Actually, Dad is insisting we stay together until she agrees to sign the revised buy/sell.

If Grandpa Schultz didn't respect my ideas, he wouldn't have left me 50% of the common.

No, it's *not* important that we understand each other. Just make sure *you* understand *me*.

Here are the statements from the accounting firm — a bit late again. It's hard to remember that far back, but looks like '65 must have been a good year.

It's a new energy source. All you have to do
is suddenly thrust two daughters-in-law
very close together.

Incompetent successors, grasping in-laws, and whimpering shareholders...

You need a diet, more exercise, a will and a successor — not necessarily in that order.

I did all I could to prepare you to take over, Son — private school, four years at Princeton, two years at Harvard Business School. Now, your first project will be to see us through Chapter 11.

You're a lot like my son, Harcourt — and you might remember that I got rid of *him*.

With all I have, I still complain...but in a higher
tax bracket, of course.

Mother wants to know when you're going to give up that business of yours and get a *real* job.

I'm afraid you have the wrong number.
However...

Fair market value only applies
when you're selling.

Of course I love your company. Uh, it *is* still
profitable, isn't it?

I'm not really sure why I don't feel comfortable
putting the business in your hands yet, Son...oh,
and by the way, those aren't folding chairs.

I've reviewed your financial situation. If we manage your money properly, there's plenty for both of us.

Just wait. It gets *really* exciting when Dad's secretary and Mom stop being nice to each other.

Harold, before you take your bath, are you sure the children have accepted your decision not to retire?

While I'm fixing dinner, why don't you and your Dad discuss our plans to make me Office Manager.

Has it occurred to you, Finkbiner, that maybe you've been with me eighteen years precisely *because* you never asked for a raise?

Okay, let's review. You say you managed to
parlay an MBA, an inherited business,
aggressive financing, and a strong taste for risk
into forced liquidation?

Danco / Jonovic — Someday It'll All Be...Who's?

But Dad's *never* invited spouses to the family shareholder meetings in Aruba!

Someday, Son, this'll all be yours and they'll pay *you* not to plant anything here.

So, tell me, when did you first notice that three times 25% equals control of the company?

Well, look at this! Memo #36 in the "It's Time We Get Something in Writing, Dad" series.

Am I to understand, Mother, that "fiddle-faddle"
and "pooh" mean you disagree?

Well...his father promised me I'd always come before
the business, too. Lying must be in the genes.

As with the previous agenda item, those who disagree
with my decision should signify by saying "I resign."

We've cut our overhead, streamlined our operation, and increased our cost-efficiency 100% in every division...this was, however, offset by bonuses, salary increases, perks, and benefits to the active shareholders.

Let's see...she's been raised, educated, married, divorced, came home, joined the business, got divorced again, left home, and now remarried. I guess our job is finished.

Edwin's taken to retirement so much better than anyone expected.

Wow! Do I own all those people?

If you don't mind, Son, I'd like to retire *before* you do.

Danco / Jonovic — Someday It'll All Be...Who's?

I get the distinct feeling that Dad's
changed his will again.

Just think, Son. Someday this will all be yours!

My father wanted me to be a partner in his business,
but the IRS got there first.

Frankly, Mr. Henderson, I've never had a man and his daughter-in-law as clients before.

I suppose it's too much to ask you to keep my job as controller open for me?

Danco / Jonovic — Someday It'll All Be...Who's?

I think I'll let absolute power corrupt me
just a tiny, little bit.

Well, how was the first day with your cousins
now that Uncle Harry and I are retired?

Danco / Jonovic — Someday It'll All Be...Who's?

Chicken? I thought you said we were gonna have the old goat for supper?

It has just occurred to me that Grandpa's generosity
with his stock may have been misguided.

Danco / Jonovic — Someday It'll All Be...Who's?

He treats me like a minority shareholder.

Before we go any further...Ms. Beechly, will you marry me?

First time I ever enjoyed something that wasn't tax deductible.

I'd like to think you would've elected me Chairman
even if Ben hadn't left me all the stock.

Face up to it, Porter. You held onto it because
nobody else wanted it.

Has it occurred to you, Edward, that working for your father was nothing more than a way to get over the hill without ever getting to the top?

Boy, am I glad I don't own this business. I've just
wasted the entire week.

For heaven's sake, John, leave the boy alone.
This is a simple pot roast, not a "result of
your blood, sweat, and tears!"

Thank you. Now get back to work.

I don't know how to tell you this, Dear, but I liked you better when you went to work every day.

I've noticed you've been with me for 30 years, Pennington. I must be losing my touch.

To quote the will exactly, it reads: "I, Amos Thornbury, being of sound mind and body, have spent it all."

No, Dad. I'm *not* pregnant yet!

Son, about your promise to smooth out the swings in the sales curve...

Nonsense, Mr. Philbeam! The whole world isn't against you. The people of the United States, perhaps, but not the whole world.

I can't tell you how pleased I was to learn that
Dad left all of us equal shares...

Then the young lad respected his father, learned from him, took over running the business without asking for control, and cheerfully supported the old guy through his dotage.